Silk

Edited by Rebecca Stefoff

Text © 1994 by Garrett Educational Corporation

First Published in the United States in 1994
by Garrett Educational Corporation,
130 East 13th Street, Ada, Oklahoma 74820.

First Published in 1991 by A & C Black Publishers Limited
with the title Silk, © 1991 A & C Black Publishers Ltd.

Manufactured in the United States of America

Library of Congress Cataloging-in-Publication Data

Deshpande, Chris.
   Silk / Chris Deshpande.
     p.   cm.—(Threads)
   Includes index.
   ISBN 1-56074-061-2
   1. Silk—Juvenile literature.   [1. Silk.]   I. Title.   II. Series.
TS1669.D47   1994
677'.39—dc20
                                                94-19350
                                                 CIP
                                                   AC

Silk

Chris Deshpande

Photographs by Prodeepta Das

Contents

GEC GARRETT EDUCATIONAL CORPORATION

Looking at silk

What is silk used for?

3

Testing silk

For thousands of years, silk thread has been woven into fabric.

With your eyes shut, compare the feel of silk with other fabrics. Which feels the softest, the smoothest? Which do you prefer?

Compare the touch of synthetic fabrics, natural fabrics, and different kinds of silk. Natural fabrics such as cotton and silk come from plants and animals. Synthetic fabrics such as nylon and polyester are made from chemicals.

How strong is silk?

Which fabric do you think is the strongest - cotton, wool or silk?

You will need

a clamp

the same size strips of silk, cotton and wool

a forcemeter

a vice

How to do it

Attach a vice to the table with a clamp. Fix the strip of silk to the forcemeter at one end and to the vice at the other end. Slowly pull until the silk tears. Look at the forcemeter to see how hard you are pulling. Try the test with the other fabrics. Which fabric is the strongest? Did you guess correctly?

The rubbing test.

You will need

the same size strips of silk and cotton

a brick

How to do it

Slowly rub the strip of fabric backwards and forwards over the brick. Count the number of rubs it takes to make each fabric tear.

How can you make sure this is a fair test?

Find out if silk is stronger than a synthetic fabric.

Did you know?

A silk thread is three times as strong as the same size thread of steel.

Does silk crease easily?

Try this "scrunchability," test to find out.

Scrunch up a piece of fine silk in one hand and a piece of cotton of the same size in the other, or ask a friend to help. What happens when you open out your hands? Which fabric is the springiest? Which fabric is the most creased? Try this test with some other fabrics.

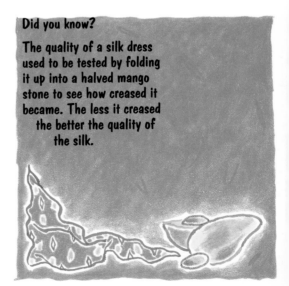

Do you think that silk should be ironed with a cool or a hot iron? Look on the dial of an iron and see what the setting is for silk.

Did you know?

The quality of a silk dress used to be tested by folding it up into a halved mango stone to see how creased it became. The less it creased the better the quality of the silk.

6

How much does silk weigh?

Which do you think weighs the most — fine silk, wool, or cotton? Try this test to find out.

You will need

spring balance or scales
pieces of wool, cotton and
silk of the same surface area

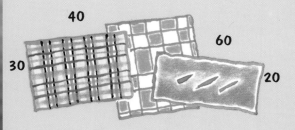

How to do it

Weigh each piece of fabric and record your results. Did you guess correctly?

Weigh different kinds of silk — fine, thick, and decorated. Do they weigh the same? Weigh a piece of fine silk and a piece of fine nylon. Which is the heaviest? Remember to make the tests fair.

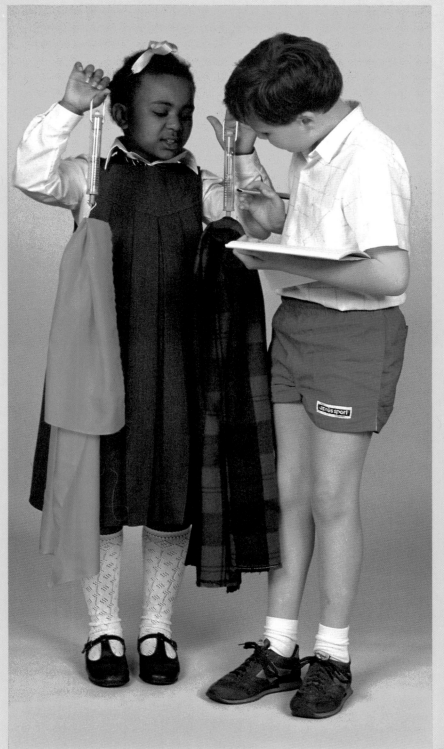

Silk for science and technology

Silk is soft, strong, and light; it can be packed into a small space and it springs back into shape quickly. These properties make silk ideal for use in science, technology, and medicine.

Silk is used to make the best computer printing ribbons.

Astronauts' clothes are made out of silk.

Doctors use silk thread for surgical stitching.

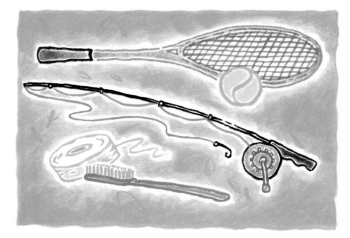

In the past, silk was used to make racket strings, fishing line, and dental floss. Can you guess why silk is not used to make these things any more?

Make your own parachute

Which fabric do you think makes the best parachute — cotton, burlap, or silk? Try this experiment to find out.

You will need

pieces of cotton, silk and burlap

a ball of string

3 equal size balls of clay

scissors

a stopwatch

How to do it

(1) Cut out a 10 inch square of cotton.

(2) Cut four 10 inch lengths of string. Attach one end of each length of string to the same ball of clay.

(3) Tie the other four ends of string to the four corners of the square. Make the silk and burlap parachutes in the same way.

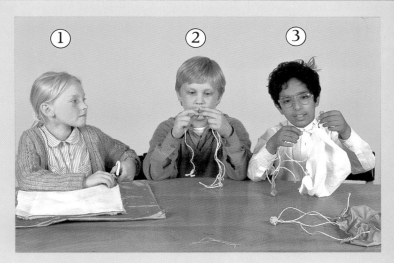

(4) Stand with the parachutes at the same height and drop them at the same time. Use a stopwatch to record how long each parachute takes to drop to the ground. Record your results.

Did you know?

In the Second World War silk parachutes were used because nylon ones were too bulky to fit into small planes.

Where does silk come from?

Most silk thread comes from the cocoon of the Bombyx mori silk moth.

When the male and female moths have mated, the female moth lays up to 500 eggs. Each egg is the size of a pin head.

Ten days later, small silkworms eat their way out of the eggs. Each silkworm is one-thirtieth of an inch long and as thick as a hair on your head.

The silkworm eats only mulberry leaves. It eats all the time and soon is too fat for its skin. For a day, it rests, stops eating, and sheds its skin. During its life, the silkworm will shed its skin four times.

Did you know?

A fully grown silkworm is about 10,000 times heavier than a newly hatched silk worm.

After seven weeks, the silkworm is fully grown and 4 inches long. The silkworm has two glands in its body, which make silk thread. The thread from each gland joins together and is sent out through a tube on its head called a spinneret. The silkworm attaches itself to a twig or frame and for three days moves its head in the shape of a figure eight, winding the thread around its body. The silkworm spins its cocoon from a single unbroken thread, which can be up to 2,000 yards long.

Inside the cocoon, the silkworm changes into a pupa. After about ten days, the pupa changes into a moth. This cycle of change is known as metamorphosis.

The moth pushes its way out of the cocoon. It rests and waits to find a mate. The silk moth cannot eat because it does not have a mouth. It cannot fly either because it has been bred in captivity for so long.

At the silk farm

For thousands of years, the Bombyx mori silk moth has been reared on silk farms in China, Japan, and India. Rearing silkworms to make silk thread is called sericulture.

The Bombyx mori silkworm will only eat the leaves of the white mulberry bush. Mulberry bushes are grown on large plantations. This machine cuts down the leaves for the silkworms to eat.

Female moths lay their eggs on large trays. When the silkworms hatch out, they are put on trays full of mulberry leaves. They are fed fresh leaves every two hours. A net covered with the fresh leaves is put over the tray. The silkworms crawl through the netting to the leaves and the net is put over a clean tray.

When the silkworms are ready to spin their cocoons, they are put on trays, which have cane frames. The silkworms attach themselves to the cane and start to spin their cocoons.

Some cocoons will be left to hatch out into moths that lay more eggs. But most of the cocoons are dried, or "stifled," in a steam room. This kills the pupa, which would have grown into a silk moth.

Did you know?

Dried pupae are full of protein and are eaten as a tasty snack.

The cocoons are graded according to size and quality. Then they are soaked in hot water to soften the sericin, or gum, that holds the cocoon together.

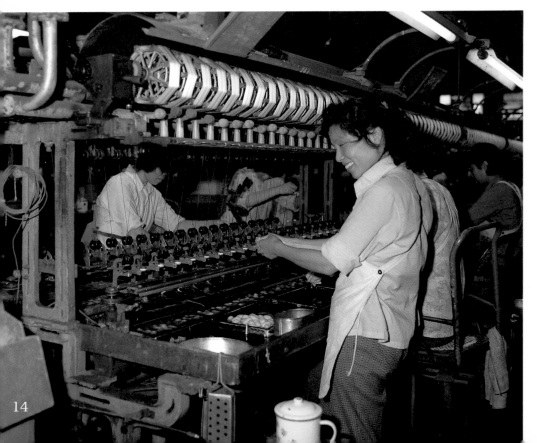

The thread from a cocoon is very fine and called a filament. The cocoon is brushed gently to catch the end of the filament. Then filaments from about eight cocoons are fed on to a reeling machine that unwinds and twists them into one thread. The sericin holds the filaments together.

The thread is wound into skeins and then collected into bundles called books. Before the thread is woven into cloth, it is twisted into thicker threads. This is called throwing. The threads are thrown to different thicknesses to make different types of silk fabric. Find out the names of some different kinds of silk fabric.

The fineness of silk thread is measured by a unit of weight called a denier. One denier is the weight of 9,000 yards of silk thread.

Good quality silk is made from the unbroken filaments of cocoons. The broken filaments are softened, combed, and twisted into shorter lengths, which are used to make spun silk.

When the silk has been twisted into thick enough threads, it is ready to be dyed different colors and woven into cloth.

15

Weaving silk into cloth

Silk thread is woven on a loom. One set of threads is stretched up and down the loom. These are the warp threads. The other set of threads runs from side to side. These are called the weft threads. This woman is working a hand loom. She uses a piece of wood called a shuttle to pass the weft threads back and forth. In big factories, the silk thread is woven into cloth on computerized looms.

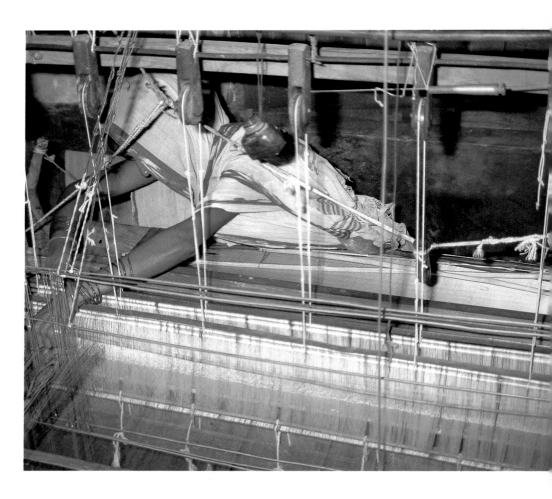

These pieces of silk cloth have been made from threads which have been dyed different colors and then woven together. Sometimes thread is woven into cloth before it is dyed, then designs are printed on to it.

Printing on silk

There are three ways of printing cloth — roller printing, block printing, and screen printing. Block printing is one of the oldest ways of printing. Try block printing a piece of cotton fabric or paper.

You will need

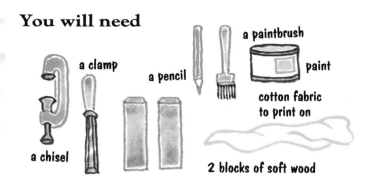

a chisel
a clamp
a pencil
a paintbrush
paint
cotton fabric to print on
2 blocks of soft wood

How to do it

○ Draw a pattern on the wood and firmly clamp the wood to the table. Carefully chisel around the pencil line so that the shape stands out, just like a potato cut. This can be dangerous so make sure an adult is nearby. Make another block in the same way.

② Paint each block a different color.

③ Press one of the blocks paint-side-down on to the fabric. Use the other block to print the other color. Go on printing little patterns until you have a big pattern.

17

Screen printing

Screen printing is another way of printing silk. Try screen printing a piece of fabric yourself. You don't have to use silk, it works just as well on cotton.

You will need

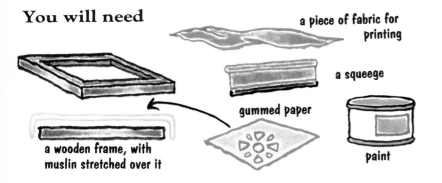

a piece of fabric for printing

a squeege

gummed paper

paint

a wooden frame, with muslin stretched over it

How to do it

①Ask an adult to help you make a wooden frame, covered with muslin. Cut out a pattern from gummed paper and stick it to the bottom of the screen. The paint will print only through the muslin; it won't print through the paper. Put the frame over the fabric and pour some paint into the end of the screen.

②Ask a friend to hold the frame while you pull the paint across the screen with the squeegee.

③Lift the frame carefully.

Roller printing is used in factories to print large amounts of material. Find out why.

18

The history of silk

There are many stories about how silk was first discovered. Some people think it was discovered 3,500 years ago by Empress Xi Lingshi of China, who was drinking tea under a mulberry bush. A white cocoon fell into the Empress' cup and when she tried to remove it, the cocoon unravelled into a fine, gleaming thread. She looked closely at the mulberry bush and saw small white silkworms spinning cocoons. She wound their thread on to reels and wove it into cloth.

The Emperor of China decreed that anyone who took the secret of how silk was made out of China would be put to death, and for over 2,000 years the secret remained there.

19

In ancient times, traders from Persia bought beautiful silks from Chinese merchants. The traders travelled to what is now Europe to sell the silk to the ancient Greeks and the Romans. They travelled on a road which was nearly 6,000 miles long and became known as the Silk Road. The road began in eastern China at Xian, ran past the Gobi Desert, and split into a northern and southern route around the Takli Makan Desert. It then ran into Central Asia and Europe.

Make up a board game, imagining you are a silk merchant travelling with a caravan of camels and cloth. What dangers do you think you will face on your journey? See page 25.

Eventually the secret of silk spread to other countries. It is said that in AD 140 a Chinese princess married an Indian prince and smuggled silk moth eggs into India in her headdress. In AD 555 two monks smuggled silk moth eggs into Europe in their bamboo walking canes.

A Chinese silk legend

This is a Chinese legend about how silk was discovered.

There was once a girl whose father was away fighting in the wars. For a long, long time she waited patiently for him to return. Then one day, as she was brushing her horse, she could stand it no longer. She exclaimed, "If someone would only bring my father back, I would marry them today." Immediately, the horse galloped off and returned with the girl's father. But when the soldier heard of his daughter's promise, he was furious. He killed the horse and left its skin to dry in the courtyard. The girl was very upset. She ran into the courtyard, where a whirlwind blew the horse's skin tightly around her. She was carried far away.

For many days, the father chased after the whirlwind, until it blew itself out in a mulberry bush. The father searched amongst the leaves and eventually found what was left of his daughter — a small white worm, which spun a fine thread. The mother and father looked after their daughter, feeding her mulberry leaves every day. They wove the thread into silk cloth.

Silk is special

In the past, only very rich or important people could afford to wear silk. Today it is still expensive and usually only worn on special occasions. This wedding dress is made out of silk. Can you think of any other celebration times when people wear silk outfits?

Silk clothes can show you what job someone does. In England, when a lawyer is made a Queen's Councillor, they swap their cotton robe for a silk one. This is called "taking silk."

Silk is used to make special things. Fine silk thread is embroidered into cushions and wall hangings, and woven into carpets. Look at this picture carefully — it has been painted on silk.

Make some silk flowers

Try and make a bunch of silk flowers for decoration.

You will need

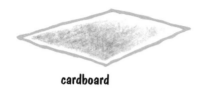
cardboard

5 10-inch lengths
of thin wire

strips of green paper

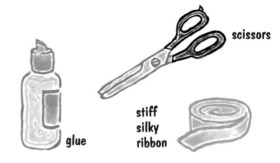
scissors

glue

stiff
silky
ribbon

How to do it

① Make a template by cutting a 3 inch long petal shape out of cardboard. Hold the template on the ribbon and cut round it.

② Stick the petal of ribbon to the top of the wire. When the glue is dry, bend the petal to curl at its tip. Make four more petals on wire stems like this.

③ Twist the five wire stems together to make one stem. Wrap sticky green paper around the stem, until it is completely covered. Make a bunch of flowers.

More things to do

1. Find out which countries produce silk and how sericulture started in these countries.

2. Joseph Jacquard invented a loom for weaving silk thread into cloth. Find out about Joseph Jacquard and his loom.

3. Find out who Louis Pasteur was and why he was important to the silk industry.

4. Silk fabric can be decorated in lots of different ways. Look at different fabrics and try to name the ways that they have been dyed, printed, and embroidered. Try decorating some fabric yourself.

5. Lots of things which were once made out of silk are now made out of nylon and other synthetic fibers. Find out what things used to be made out of silk.

6. This book has told you about silk thread that comes from the Bombyx mori silkworm. See if you can find out about some other kinds of silkworms that spin silk thread.

7. How to make the Silk Road game: on a large piece of paper, draw a long winding road and mark it off into squares. Mark the first square as the place Xian and the last square as your home town. Mark some of the squares in between with the names of towns on the Silk Road. Color some squares red, some green and one square with stripes. For the red squares think of things that will slow down your journey, such as — you are attacked by robbers, or you reach an oasis but it is dry. For the green squares think of things which will speed up your journey. For the striped square think of a reason why you might have to go back to Xian.

How to play the Silk Road game: for two players you will need two counters, dice, a map of the world, drawing pins and some ribbon. Throw the dice in turn and move your counters on the board by the number thrown. If you land on a red square, go back two spaces. If you land on a green square, go forward two spaces. When you land on the striped square, go back to the beginning. When you reach a town, pin the ribbon to that town on the map. The winner is the first one home.

Index

(Numbers in **bold** type are pages that show activities.)